Zoom in on
INDUSTRIAL ROBOTS

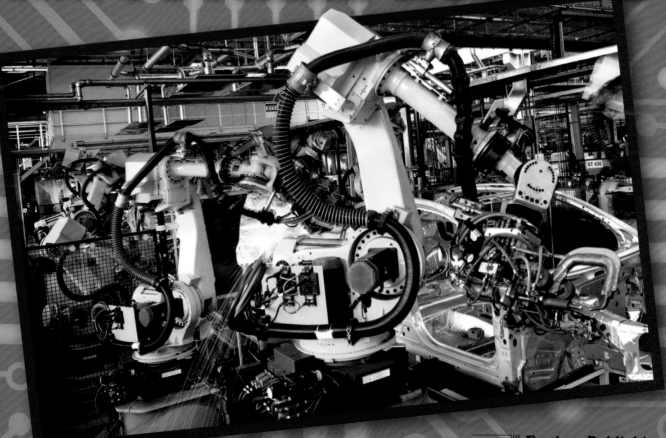

Enslow Publishing
101 W. 23rd Street
Suite 240
New York, NY 10011
USA

enslow.com

Sara L. Latta

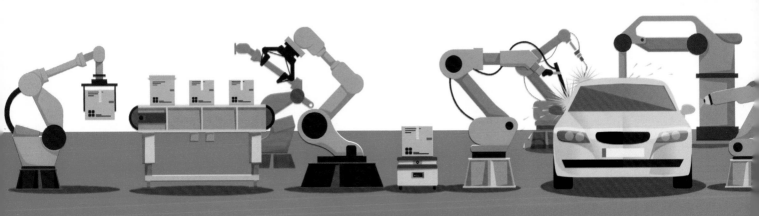

WORDS TO KNOW

assembly   The act of putting something together.

factory   A place where products are made.

industrial   Having to do with making things.

microscope   An instrument that makes tiny things look larger.

sensor   A part of a robot that helps it understand the world around it.

warehouse   A building made for storing goods.

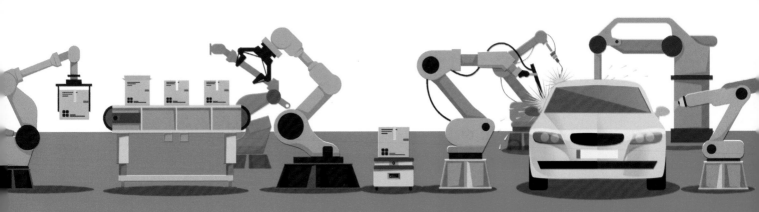

CONTENTS

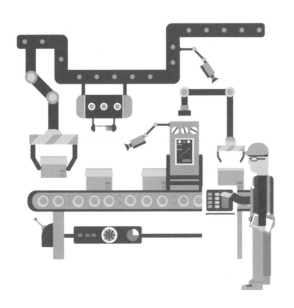

Industrial Robots

Industrial robots work in factories. They build cars and computers. They labor in warehouses. They carry heavy loads. Robots can do the same job over and over again. They do not get tired. They work fast. They rarely make mistakes.

Robots can do jobs that are unsafe or boring for humans. But factories still need people to oversee the robots.

A robot arm can move part of a washing machine.

What Are Robots?

Robots are machines. They can do jobs by themselves. Computers tell robots what to do. Robots have parts that let the robot move. They can grab, turn, or lift. They have sensors. Cameras and microphones tell them about things nearby.

What Do Industrial Robots Look Like?

Most industrial robots do not look like people. They come in many shapes and sizes. Some have huge arms that can lift an entire car. Medium-

Arm Power

The first industrial robot went to work in 1961. The robot had a giant arm. It took parts from an assembly line and put them on cars.

A robot places a pizza in the oven.

sized robots make computers or even pizzas. Still other
robots are smaller than a human cell. You would need a
microscope to see them!

8

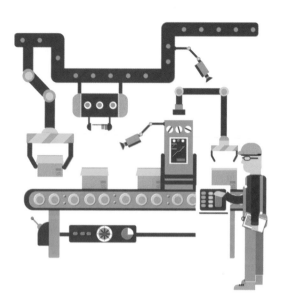

Robot Builders

Many companies use assembly lines to make their goods. Assembly lines make it possible to make many items quickly. At a car factory, the frame might be the first thing to enter the line. A belt moves it to the first workstation. Here, robots attach the front doors. The frame moves to the next station. Other robots attach the back doors. Robots add more parts as the car moves from one station to the next.

Robots weld parts to cars in a factory. It is a dangerous job for humans, but not for robots.

The one-armed robots used in car factories swing their arms to build and move materials. It is dangerous for people to work near these robots.

Robots That Work with Humans

There is a new kind of industrial robot. It can work with people. A robot called Baxter uses sensors to find objects. It grabs them with its "hands." It is easy for people to program Baxter to carry out a

Fast Cars

In 1913, Henry Ford built the first moving assembly line to make cars. It allowed his human workers to make cars faster and cheaper than ever before.

new task. They just move its arms to show it how to do a job.

Baxter is good at picking things up and putting them down. It can deal with sudden changes, like finding a missing part. Baxter cannot hurt human workers by accident. If Baxter bumps into somebody, it backs away. Baxter works with human factory workers to build more things faster.

The Baxter robot can grab items. Humans program Baxter to carry out new tasks.

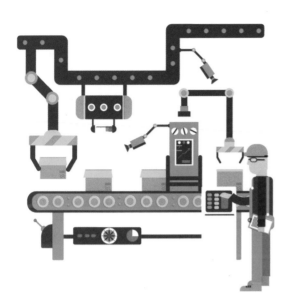

Robot Testers and Workers

EARL is an expert bowler. Time after time, EARL's bowling ball knocks down all of the pins at the end of the alley. EARL can throw the ball fast or slow. EARL is a robot. It can copy any bowling style. EARL's job is testing new bowling gear.

This robot is spray painting machine parts.

Robots Do the Hard Work

Imagine testing a new dishwasher. You put in the dish soap. You load the dirty dishes. You turn on the dishwasher and wait. You unload the dishwasher. Then you do it all over again. It is boring and hard work for a human. Robot testers can do it 24 hours a day, 7 days a week. They work along with humans to get the job done.

One van maker uses robot-driven cars to test for safety and sturdiness. The robots drive the

Testing

Companies use robot testers to make sure their products can handle the wear and tear of regular use. They must show that their products are safe.

vans on specially made courses. The courses are rough. People can drive them only once a day. The robot can drive the courses many times in one day.

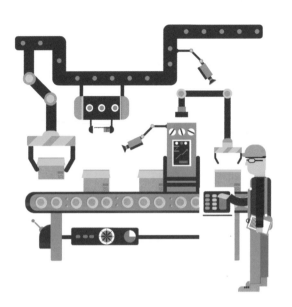

Robots Carry Heavy Loads

Large companies store their products in huge warehouses. The warehouses can hold millions of items. The items are stored there until a customer wants to buy them. In the past, warehouse workers might have walked many miles each day to fetch toys, books, or other goods. Now, many warehouses use robots to fetch and deliver these items to workers.

A robot can move large pieces of steel in this warehouse.

The Lego factory in Denmark uses robots to carry loads of plastic bricks around the workplace. The loads are too heavy for people to carry. The robot has sensors that tell it to stop before it would hit a human worker.

Will Robots Take Away Jobs for People?

Some people worry that robots will take jobs from factory and warehouse workers. Experts agree. But many experts also say that the use of robots will open up new jobs for people.

Robots at Work

The US Census Bureau estimates that robots will take over five million jobs now held by humans by the year 2020.

19

An engineer programs a robot's computer.

We might not even know what they are yet. A farmer living in the nineteenth century could not have imagined the job of computer programmer.

Robots may take over many dirty, dangerous, or boring jobs. But they cannot take over interesting jobs that require creative thinking.

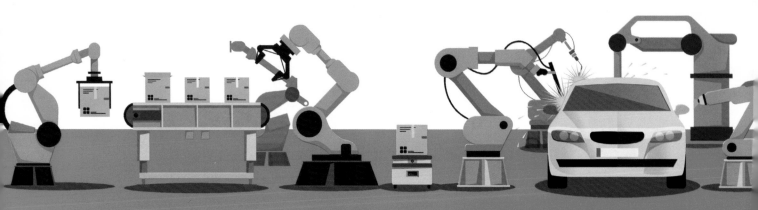

ACTIVITY:
PROGRAM A ROBOT

You learned how factories use robots in assembly lines to make things. Now you and your friends will form your own assembly lines. You get to play the part of the robots. You can make anything you want. Here is one suggestion: cars that you can eat. The goal is to make the most cars in the shortest time. But remember: they have to be very well made. If they are not, they get thrown out!

What you'll need:

paper plates

graham crackers

frosting

round candies, such as Life-Savers®

chocolate bars (the kind that can be broken into small rectangles)

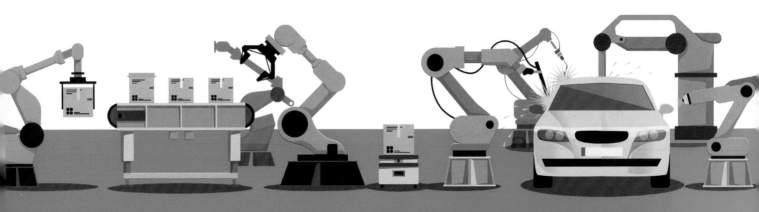

What you'll do:

1. Form at least two teams of five people each. These teams will play the role of robots on an assembly line. Another team of at least two people will be in charge of quality control.

2. Each graham cracker serves as the body of the car. The frosting is the "glue" that holds the parts together. The round candies are the wheels. The chocolate bars are the windows.

3. The quality control team decides how the car should look. Where should the wheels be? How about the windows? How much frosting should be used?

4. Each assembly team decides how to set up their line. Remember, each member of the team is a robot. They can only do one task at a time. What is the best way to assemble the car?

5. Go! Each assembly line works to make their cars quickly. They must make them well. What is the best way to make good cars in the shortest time? The judges decide!

LEARN MORE

Books

Schulman, Mark. *TIME for Kids Explorers: Robots.* New York, NY: TIME for Kids, 2014.

Stewart, Melissa. *National Geographic Readers: Robots.* Washington, DC: National Geographic Children's Books, 2014.

Tuchman, Gail. *Robots.* New York, NY: Scholastic, 2015.

Websites

Robotics: Facts
idahoptv.org/sciencetrek/topics/robots/facts.cfm
Check out many interesting facts about robots.

Robots for Kids
sciencekids.co.nz/robots.html
Check out the world of robots with games, facts, projects, quizzes, and videos.

INDEX

Published in 2018 by Enslow Publishing, LLC.
101 W. 23rd Street, Suite 240, New York, NY 10011

Library of Congress Cataloging-in-Publication Data
Names: Latta, Sara L., author.
Title: Zoom in on industrial robots / Sara L. Latta.
Description: New York : Enslow Publishing, 2018. | Series: Zoom in on robots | Includes bibliographical references and index.
Identifiers: LCCN 2017021475| ISBN 9780766092266 (library bound) | ISBN 9780766094369 (pbk.) | ISBN 9780766094376 (6 pack)
Subjects: LCSH: Robots, Industrial—Juvenile literature.
Classification: LCC TS191.8 .L375 2018 | DDC 629.8/92—dc23
LC record available at https://lccn.loc.gov/2017021475

Printed in the United States of America

To Our Readers: We have done our best to make sure all website addresses in this book were active and appropriate when we went to press. However, the author and the publisher have no control over and assume no liability for the material available on those websites or on any websites they may link to. Any comments or suggestions can be sent by email to customerservice@enslow.com.

Photos Credits: Cover, p. 1 Rainer Plendl/Shutterstock.com; p. 4 Tim Johnson/MCT/Tribune News Services/Getty Images; p. 6 Matthew Lloyd/Bloomberg/Getty Images; p. 8 © AP Images; p. 10 wi6995/Shutterstock.com; p. 12 Nicky Loh/Bloomberg/Getty Images; p. 14, 18 Monty Rakusen/Cultura/Getty Images; p. 16 Jeff Kowalsky/Bloomberg/Getty Images; p. 20 Hero Images/Getty Images; p. 22 (cracker) Duplass/Shutterstock.com, (candy) oksana2010/Shutterstock.com, (chocolate bar) Drozzhina Elena/Shutterstock.com; graphic elements Cover, p. 1 (background) Perzeus/Shutterstock.com, pp. 2, 3, 22, 23 Macrovector/Shutterstock.com, pp. 5, 9, 13, 17 LineTale/Shutterstock.com.